BY ADRIENNE RICH

Dark Fields of the Republic

What is Found There: Notebooks on Poetry and Politics

Collected Early Poems 1950–1970

An Atlas of the Difficult World
Poems 1988–1991

Time's Power: Poems 1985–1988

Blood, Bread, and Poetry: Selected Prose 1979–1986

Your Native Land, Your Life

The Fact of a Doorframe: Poems Selected and New 1950–1984

Sources

A Wild Patience Has Taken Me This Far

On Lies, Secrets, and Silence: Selected Prose, 1966–1978

The Dream of a Common Language

Twenty-one Love Poems

Of Woman Born: Motherhood as Experience and Institution

Poems: Selected and New, 1950–1974

Diving into the Wreck

The Will to Change

Leaflets

Necessities of Life

Snapshots of a Daughter-in-Law

The Diamond Cutters

A Change of World

THE DREAM
OF A
COMMON
LANGUAGE

POEMS 1974-1977

W · W · NORTON & COMPANY

New York · London

THE DREAM
OF A
COMMON
LANGUAGE

POEMS 1974-1977

ADRIENNE RICH

W. W. Norton & Company, Inc., 500 Fifth Avenue, New York, NY 10110
W. W. Norton & Company Ltd., 10 Coptic Street, London WC1A 1PU

Norton paperback reissue 1993.

Printed in the United States of America.

Some of these poems originally appeared in the following periodicals: *Amazon Quarterly, Chrysalis, College English, Field, Heresies, The Little Magazine, Moving Out, Ms., New Boston Review, Sinister Wisdom, 13th Moon.*

Twenty-one Love Poems was first published in a limited edition, designed and hand-printed by Bonnie Carpenter at Effie's Press, Emeryville, California.

Some phrases in the poem "Paula Becker to Clara Westhoff" are quoted from actual diaries and letters of Paula Modersohn-Becker, as translated by Liselotte Erlanger. As yet, no English edition of the Modersohn-Becker manuscript exists.

BOOK DESIGN BY ANTONINA KRASS
TYPEFACES USED ARE JANSON AND V.I.P. ELECTRA
MANUFACTURED BY MAPLE-VAIL BOOK MANUFACTURING GROUP

Library of Congress Cataloging in Publication Data
Rich, Adrienne.
    The dream of a common language.
    "Twenty-one love poems": p.
    1. Women—Poetry. I. Rich. Adrienne.
Twenty-one love poems. 1978. II. Title.
PS3535.I233D7   1978   811'.5'4   77-28156
ISBN 0-393-31033-7

7 8 9 0

I go where I love and where I am loved,
into the snow;

I go to the things I love
with no thought of duty or pity

—H. D. *The Flowering of the Rod*

CONTENTS

I
POWER

II
TWENTY-ONE LOVE POEMS

III

NOT SOMEWHERE ELSE,
BUT HERE

I

POWER

POWER

Living   in the earth-deposits   of our history

Today a backhoe divulged   out of a crumbling flank of earth
one bottle   amber   perfect   a hundred-year-old
cure for fever   or melancholy   a tonic
for living on this earth   in the winters of this climate

Today I was reading about Marie Curie:
she must have known she suffered   from radiation sickness
her body bombarded for years   by the element
she had purified
It seems she denied to the end
the source of the cataracts on her eyes
the cracked and suppurating skin   of her finger-ends
till she could no longer hold   a test-tube or a pencil

She died   a famous woman   denying
her wounds
denying
her wounds   came   from the same source as her power

1974

PHANTASIA FOR ELVIRA SHATAYEV

(leader of a women's climbing team, all of whom died in a
storm on Lenin Peak, August 1974. Later, Shatayev's
husband found and buried the bodies.)

The cold felt cold until our blood
grew colder   then the wind
died down and we slept

If in this sleep I speak
it's with a voice no longer personal
(I want to say   *with voices*)
When the wind tore   our breath from us at last
we had no need of words
For months   for years   each one of us
had felt her own *yes*   growing in her
slowly forming   as she stood at windows   waited
for trains   mended her rucksack   combed her hair
What we were to learn   was simply   what we had
up here   as out of all words   that *yes*   gathered
its forces   fused itself   and only just in time
to meet a No of no degrees
the black hole   sucking the world in

I feel you climbing toward me
your cleated bootsoles leaving   their geometric bite
colossally embossed   on microscopic crystals
as when I trailed you in the Caucasus
Now I am further
ahead   than either of us dreamed   anyone would be
I have become

the white snow packed like asphalt by the wind
the women I love   lightly flung   against the mountain
that blue sky
our frozen eyes unribboned   through the storm
we could have stitched that blueness   together   like a quilt

You come (I know this)   with your love   your loss
strapped to your body   with your tape-recorder   camera
ice-pick   against advisement
to give us burial in the snow   and in your mind
While my body lies out here
flashing like a prism   into your eyes
how could you sleep   You climbed here for yourself
we climbed for ourselves

When you have buried us   told your story
ours does not end   we stream
into the unfinished   the unbegun
the possible
Every cell's core of heat   pulsed out of us
into the thin air   of the universe
the armature of rock beneath these snows
this mountain   which has taken   the imprint of our minds
through changes elemental and minute
as those we underwent
to bring each other here
choosing ourselves   each other   and this life
whose every breath   and grasp   and further foothold
is somewhere   still enacted   and continuing

In the diary I wrote: *Now we are ready*
and each of us knows it   I have never loved
like this   I have never seen
my own forces so taken up and shared
and given back

After the long training   the early sieges
we are moving almost effortlessly in our love

In the diary as the wind   began to tear
at the tents over us   I wrote:
We know now we have always been in danger
down in our separateness
and now up here together   but till now
we had not touched our strength

In the diary torn from my fingers I had written:
What does love mean
what does it mean   "to survive"
A cable of blue fire ropes our bodies
burning together in the snow   We will not live
to settle for less   We have dreamed of this
all of our lives

1974

ORIGINS AND HISTORY
OF CONSCIOUSNESS

I

Night-life. Letters, journals, bourbon
sloshed in the glass. Poems crucified on the wall,
dissected, their bird-wings severed
like trophies. No one lives in this room
without living through some kind of crisis.

No one lives in this room
without confronting the whiteness of the wall
behind the poems, planks of books,
photographs of dead heroines.
Without contemplating last and late
the true nature of poetry. The drive
to connect. The dream of a common language.

Thinking of lovers, their blind faith, their
experienced crucifixions,
my envy is not simple. I have dreamed of going to bed
as walking into clear water ringed by a snowy wood
white as cold sheets, thinking, *I'll freeze in there.*
My bare feet are numbed already by the snow
but the water
is mild, I sink and float
like a warm amphibious animal
that has broken the net, has run
through fields of snow leaving no print;
this water washes off the scent—
You are clear now

of the hunter, the trapper
the wardens of the mind—

yet the warm animal dreams on
of another animal
swimming under the snow-flecked surface of the pool,
and wakes, and sleeps again.

No one sleeps in this room without
the dream of a common language.

II

It was simple to meet you, simple to take your eyes
into mine, saying: these are eyes I have known
from the first. . . . It was simple to touch you
against the hacked background, the grain of what we
had been, the choices, years. . . . It was even simple
to take each other's lives in our hands, as bodies.

What is not simple: to wake from drowning
from where the ocean beat inside us like an afterbirth
into this common, acute particularity
these two selves who walked half a lifetime untouching—
to wake to something deceptively simple: a glass
sweated with dew, a ring of the telephone, a scream
of someone beaten up far down in the street
causing each of us to listen to her own inward scream

knowing the mind of the mugger and the mugged
as any woman must who stands to survive this city,
this century, this life . . .

each of us having loved the flesh in its clenched or loosened beauty
better than trees or music (yet loving those too
as if they were flesh—and they are—but the flesh
of beings unfathomed as yet in our roughly literal life).

III

It's simple to wake from sleep with a stranger,
dress, go out, drink coffee,
enter a life again. It isn't simple
to wake from sleep into the neighborhood
of one neither strange nor familiar
whom we have chosen to trust. Trusting, untrusting,
we lowered ourselves into this, let ourselves
downward hand over hand as on a rope that quivered
over the unscarched. . . . We did this. Conceived
of each other, conceived each other in a darkness
which I remember as drenched in light.
                                        I want to call this, life.

But I can't call it life until we start to move
beyond this secret circle of fire
where our bodies are giant shadows flung on a wall
where the night becomes our inner darkness, and sleeps
like a dumb beast, head on her paws, in the corner.

1972–1974

SPLITTINGS

1.

My body opens over San Francisco like the day-
light raining down   each pore crying the change of light
I am not with her   I have been waking off and on
all night to that pain   not simply absence but
the presence of the past   destructive
to living here and now   Yet if I could instruct
myself, if we could learn to learn from pain
even as it grasps us   if the mind, the mind that lives
in this body could refuse   to let itself be crushed
in that grasp   it would loosen   Pain would have to stand
off from me and listen   its dark breath still on me
but the mind could begin to speak to pain
and pain would have to answer:

                                We are older now
we have met before   these are my hands before your eyes
my figure blotting out   all that is not mine
I am the pain of division   creator of divisions
it is I who blot your lover from you
and not the time-zones nor the miles
It is not separation calls me forth   but I
who am separation   And remember
I have no existence   apart from you

2.

I believe I am choosing something new
not to suffer uselessly   yet still to feel
Does the infant memorize the body of the mother
and create her in absence?   or simply cry
primordial loneliness?   does the bed of the stream
once diverted   mourning   remember wetness?

But we, we live so much in these
configurations of the past   I choose
to separate her   from my past we have not shared
I choose not to suffer uselessly
to detect primordial pain as it stalks toward me
flashing its bleak torch in my eyes   blotting out
her particular being   the details of her love
I will not be divided   from her or from myself
by myths of separation
while her mind and body in Manhattan are more with me
than the smell of eucalyptus coolly burning   on these hills

3.
The world tells me I am its creature
I am raked by eyes   brushed by hands
I want to crawl into her for refuge   lay my head
in the space   between her breast and shoulder
abnegating power for love
as women have done   or hiding
from power in her love   like a man
I refuse these givens   the splitting
between love and action   I am choosing
not to suffer uselessly   and not to use her
I choose to love   this time   for once
with all my intelligence

1974

HUNGER

(FOR AUDRE LORDE)

1.

A fogged hill-scene on an enormous continent,
intimacy rigged with terrors,
a sequence of blurs the Chinese painter's ink-stick planned,
a scene of desolation comforted
by two human figures recklessly exposed,
leaning together in a sticklike boat
in the foreground. Maybe we look like this,
I don't know. I'm wondering
whether we even have what we think we have—
lighted windows signifying shelter,
a film of domesticity
over fragile roofs. I know I'm partly somewhere else—
huts strung across a drought-stretched land
not mine, dried breasts, mine and not mine, a mother
watching my children shrink with hunger.
I live in my Western skin,
my Western vision, torn
and flung to what I can't control or even fathom.
Quantify suffering, you could rule the world.

2.

They cán rule the world while they can persuade us
our pain belongs in some order.
Is death by famine worse than death by suicide,
than a life of famine and suicide, if a black lesbian dies,
if a white prostitute dies, if a woman genius
starves herself to feed others,
self-hatred battening on her body?
Something that kills us or leaves us half-alive
is raging under the name of an "act of god"

in Chad, in Niger, in the Upper Volta—
yes, that male god that acts on us and on our children,
that male State that acts on us and on our children
till our brains are blunted by malnutrition,
yet sharpened by the passion for survival,
our powers expended daily on the struggle
to hand a kind of life on to our children,
to change reality for our lovers
even in a single trembling drop of water.

3.
We can look at each other through both our lifetimes
like those two figures in the sticklike boat
flung together in the Chinese ink-scene;
even our intimacies are rigged with terror.
Quantify suffering? My guilt at least is open,
I stand convicted by all my convictions—
you, too. We shrink from touching
our power, we shrink away, we starve ourselves
and each other, we're scared shitless
of what it could be to take and use our love,
hose it on a city, on a world,
to wield and guide its spray, destroying
poisons, parasites, rats, viruses—
like the terrible mothers we long and dread to be.

4.
The decision to feed the world
is the real decision. No revolution
has chosen it. For that choice requires
that women shall be free.
I choke on the taste of bread in North America
but the taste of hunger in North America
is poisoning me. Yes, I'm alive to write these words,
to leaf through Kollwitz's women

huddling the stricken children into their stricken arms
the "mothers" drained of milk, the "survivors" driven
to self-abortion, self-starvation, to a vision
bitter, concrete, and wordless.
I'm alive to want more than life,
want it for others starving and unborn,
to name the deprivations boring
into my will, my affections, into the brains
of daughters, sisters, lovers caught in the crossfire
of terrorists of the mind.
In the black mirror of the subway window
hangs my own face, hollow with anger and desire.
Swathed in exhaustion, on the trampled newsprint,
a woman shields a dead child from the camera.
The passion to be inscribes her body.
Until we find each other, we are alone.

1974–1975

TO A POET

Ice splits   under the metal
shovel   another day
hazed light off fogged panes
cruelty of winter   landlocked   your life
wrapped round you   in your twenties
an old bathrobe   dragged down
with milkstains   tearstains   dust

Scraping eggcrust from the child's
dried dish   skimming the skin
from cooled milk   wringing diapers
Language floats at the vanishing-point
incarnate   breathes the fluorescent bulb
primary   states the scarred grain of the floor
and on the ceiling in torn plaster laughs   *imago*

> *and I have fears that you will cease to be*
> *before your pen has glean'd your teeming brain*

for you are not a suicide
but no-one calls this murder
Small mouths, needy, suck you: *This is love*

I write this   not for you
who fight to write your own
words   fighting up the falls
but for another woman   dumb
with loneliness   dust   seeping plastic bags
with children   in a house
where language floats and spins
abortion   in
the bowl

1974

CARTOGRAPHIES OF SILENCE

1.
A conversation begins
with a lie. And each

speaker of the so-called common language feels
the ice-floe split, the drift apart

as if powerless, as if up against
a force of nature

A poem can begin
with a lie. And be torn up.

A conversation has other laws
recharges itself with its own

false energy. Cannot be torn
up. Infiltrates our blood. Repeats itself.

Inscribes with its unreturning stylus
the isolation it denies.

2.
The classical music station
playing hour upon hour in the apartment

the picking up and picking up
and again picking up the telephone

The syllables uttering
the old script over and over

The loneliness of the liar
living in the formal network of the lie

twisting the dials to drown the terror
beneath the unsaid word

3.
The technology of silence
The rituals, etiquette

the blurring of terms
silence not absence

of words or music or even
raw sounds

Silence can be a plan
rigorously executed

the blueprint to a life

It is a presence
it has a history   a form

Do not confuse it
with any kind of absence

4.
How calm, how inoffensive these words
begin to seem to me

though begun in grief and anger
Can I break through this film of the abstract

without wounding myself or you

there is enough pain here

This is why the classical or the jazz music station plays?
to give a ground of meaning to our pain?

5.
The silence that strips bare:
In Dreyer's *Passion of Joan*

Falconetti's face, hair shorn, a great geography
mutely surveyed by the camera

If there were a poetry where this could happen
not as blank spaces or as words

stretched like a skin over meanings
but as silence falls at the end

of a night through which two people
have talked till dawn

6.
The scream
of an illegitimate voice

It has ceased to hear itself, therefore
it asks itself

How do I exist?

This was the silence I wanted to break in you
I had questions but you would not answer

I had answers but you could not use them
This is useless to you and perhaps to others

7.
It was an old theme even for me:
Language cannot do everything—

chalk it on the walls where the dead poets
lie in their mausoleums

If at the will of the poet the poem
could turn into a thing

a granite flank laid bare, a lifted head
alight with dew

If it could simply look you in the face
with naked eyeballs, not letting you turn

till you, and I who long to make this thing,
were finally clarified together in its stare

8.
No. Let me have this dust,
these pale clouds dourly lingering, these words

moving with ferocious accuracy
like the blind child's fingers

or the newborn infant's mouth
violent with hunger

No one can give me, I have long ago
taken this method

whether of bran pouring from the loose-woven sack

or of the bunsen-flame turned low and blue

If from time to time I envy
the pure annunciations to the eye

the *visio beatifica*
if from time to time I long to turn

like the Eleusinian hierophant
holding up a simple ear of grain

for return to the concrete and everlasting world
what in fact I keep choosing

are these words, these whispers, conversations
from which time after time the truth breaks moist and green.

1975

THE LIONESS

The scent of her beauty draws me to her place.
The desert stretches, edge from edge.
Rock. Silver grasses. Drinking-hole.
The starry sky.
The lioness pauses
in her back-and-forth pacing of three yards square
and looks at me. Her eyes
are truthful. They mirror rivers,
seacoasts, volcanoes, the warmth
of moon-bathed promontories.
Under her haunches' golden hide
flows an innate, half-abnegated power.
Her walk
is bounded. Three square yards
encompass where she goes.

In country like this, I say, *the problem is always*
one of straying too far, not of staying
within bounds. There are caves,
high rocks, you don't explore. Yet you know
they exist. Her proud, vulnerable head
sniffs toward them. It is her country, she
knows they exist.

I come towards her in the starlight.
I look into her eyes
as one who loves can look,
entering the space behind her eyeballs,
leaving myself outside.
So, at last, through her pupils,

I see what she is seeing:
between her and the river's flood,
the volcano veiled in rainbow,
a pen that measures three yards square.
Lashed bars.
The cage.
The penance.

1975

II

TWENTY-ONE
LOVE POEMS

I

Wherever in this city, screens flicker
with pornography, with science-fiction vampires,
victimized hirelings bending to the lash,
we also have to walk . . . if simply as we walk
through the rainsoaked garbage, the tabloid cruelties
of our own neighborhoods.
We need to grasp our lives inseparable
from those rancid dreams, that blurt of metal, those disgraces,
and the red begonia perilously flashing
from a tenement sill six stories high,
or the long-legged young girls playing ball
in the junior highschool playground.
No one has imagined us. We want to live like trees,
sycamores blazing through the sulfuric air,
dappled with scars, still exuberantly budding,
our animal passion rooted in the city.

II

I wake up in your bed. I know I have been dreaming.
Much earlier, the alarm broke us from each other,
you've been at your desk for hours. I know what I dreamed:
our friend the poet comes into my room
where I've been writing for days,
drafts, carbons, poems are scattered everywhere,
and I want to show her one poem
which is the poem of my life. But I hesitate,
and wake. You've kissed my hair
to wake me. *I dreamed you were a poem,*
I say, *a poem I wanted to show someone . . .*
and I laugh and fall dreaming again
of the desire to show you to everyone I love,
to move openly together
in the pull of gravity, which is not simple,
which carries the feathered grass a long way down the upbreathing air.

III

Since we're not young, weeks have to do time
for years of missing each other. Yet only this odd warp
in time tells me we're not young.
Did I ever walk the morning streets at twenty,
my limbs streaming with a purer joy?
did I lean from any window over the city
listening for the future
as I listen here with nerves tuned for your ring?
And you, you move toward me with the same tempo.
Your eyes are everlasting, the green spark
of the blue-eyed grass of early summer,
the green-blue wild cress washed by the spring.
At twenty, yes: we thought we'd live forever.
At forty-five, I want to know even our limits.
I touch you knowing we weren't born tomorrow,
and somehow, each of us will help the other live,
and somewhere, each of us must help the other die.

IV

I come home from you through the early light of spring
flashing off ordinary walls, the Pez Dorado,
the Discount Wares, the shoe-store. . . . I'm lugging my sack
of groceries, I dash for the elevator
where a man, taut, elderly, carefully composed
lets the door almost close on me. —*For god's sake hold it!*
I croak at him. —*Hysterical,*— he breathes my way.
I let myself into the kitchen, unload my bundles,
make coffee, open the window, put on Nina Simone
singing *Here comes the sun.* . . . I open the mail,
drinking delicious coffee, delicious music,
my body still both light and heavy with you. The mail
lets fall a Xerox of something written by a man
aged 27, a hostage, tortured in prison:

My genitals have been the object of such a sadistic display
they keep me constantly awake with the pain . . .
Do whatever you can to survive.
You know, I think that men love wars . . .
And my incurable anger, my unmendable wounds
break open further with tears, I am crying helplessly,
and they still control the world, and you are not in my arms.

V

This apartment full of books could crack open
to the thick jaws, the bulging eyes
of monsters, easily: Once open the books, you have to face
the underside of everything you've loved—
the rack and pincers held in readiness, the gag
even the best voices have had to mumble through,
the silence burying unwanted children—
women, deviants, witnesses—in desert sand.
Kenneth tells me he's been arranging his books
so he can look at Blake and Kafka while he types;
yes; and we still have to reckon with Swift
loathing the woman's flesh while praising her mind,
Goethe's dread of the Mothers, Claudel vilifying Gide,
and the ghosts—their hands clasped for centuries—
of artists dying in childbirth, wise-women charred at the stake,
centuries of books unwritten piled behind these shelves;
and we still have to stare into the absence
of men who would not, women who could not, speak
to our life—this still unexcavated hole
called civilization, this act of translation, this half-world.

VI

Your small hands, precisely equal to my own—
only the thumb is larger, longer—in these hands

I could trust the world, or in many hands like these,
handling power-tools or steering-wheel
or touching a human face. . . . Such hands could turn
the unborn child rightways in the birth canal
or pilot the exploratory rescue-ship
through icebergs, or piece together
the fine, needle-like sherds of a great krater-cup
bearing on its sides
figures of ecstatic women striding
to the sibyl's den or the Eleusinian cave—
such hands might carry out an unavoidable violence
with such restraint, with such a grasp
of the range and limits of violence
that violence ever after would be obsolete.

VII

What kind of beast would turn its life into words?
What atonement is this all about?
—and yet, writing words like these, I'm also living.
Is all this close to the wolverines' howled signals,
that modulated cantata of the wild?
or, when away from you I try to create you in words,
am I simply using you, like a river or a war?
And how have I used rivers, how have I used wars
to escape writing of the worst thing of all—
not the crimes of others, not even our own death,
but the failure to want our freedom passionately enough
so that blighted elms, sick rivers, massacres would seem
mere emblems of that desecration of ourselves?

VIII

I can see myself years back at Sunion,
hurting with an infected foot, Philoctetes
in woman's form, limping the long path,

lying on a headland over the dark sea,
looking down the red rocks to where a soundless curl
of white told me a wave had struck,
imagining the pull of that water from that height,
knowing deliberate suicide wasn't my métier,
yet all the time nursing, measuring that wound.
Well, that's finished. The woman who cherished
her suffering is dead. I am her descendant.
I love the scar-tissue she handed on to me,
but I want to go on from here with you
fighting the temptation to make a career of pain.

IX

Your silence today is a pond where drowned things live
I want to see raised dripping and brought into the sun.
It's not my own face I see there, but other faces,
even your face at another age.
Whatever's lost there is needed by both of us—
a watch of old gold, a water-blurred fever chart,
a key. . . . Even the silt and pebbles of the bottom
deserve their glint of recognition. I fear this silence,
this inarticulate life. I'm waiting
for a wind that will gently open this sheeted water
for once, and show me what I can do
for you, who have often made the unnameable
nameable for others, even for me.

X

Your dog, tranquil and innocent, dozes through
our cries, our murmured dawn conspiracies
our telephone calls. She knows—what can she know?
If in my human arrogance I claim to read
her eyes, I find there only my own animal thoughts:
that creatures must find each other for bodily comfort,

that voices of the psyche drive through the flesh
further than the dense brain could have foretold,
that the planetary nights are growing cold for those
on the same journey who want to touch
one creature-traveler clear to the end;
that without tenderness, we are in hell.

XI

Every peak is a crater. This is the law of volcanoes,
making them eternally and visibly female.
No height without depth, without a burning core,
though our straw soles shred on the hardened lava.
I want to travel with you to every sacred mountain
smoking within like the sibyl stooped over her tripod,
I want to reach for your hand as we scale the path,
to feel your arteries glowing in my clasp,
never failing to note the small, jewel-like flower
unfamiliar to us, nameless till we rename her,
that clings to the slowly altering rock—
that detail outside ourselves that brings us to ourselves,
was here before us, knew we would come, and sees beyond us.

XII

Sleeping, turning in turn like planets
rotating in their midnight meadow:
a touch is enough to let us know
we're not alone in the universe, even in sleep:
the dream-ghosts of two worlds
walking their ghost-towns, almost address each other.
I've wakened to your muttered words
spoken light- or dark-years away
as if my own voice had spoken.
But we have different voices, even in sleep,
and our bodies, so alike, are yet so different

and the past echoing through our bloodstreams
is freighted with different language, different meanings—
though in any chronicle of the world we share
it could be written with new meaning
we were two lovers of one gender,
we were two women of one generation.

XIII

The rules break like a thermometer,
quicksilver spills across the charted systems,
we're out in a country that has no language
no laws, we're chasing the raven and the wren
through gorges unexplored since dawn
whatever we do together is pure invention
the maps they gave us were out of date
by years . . . we're driving through the desert
wondering if the water will hold out
the hallucinations turn to simple villages
the music on the radio comes clear—
neither *Rosenkavalier* nor *Götterdämmerung*
but a woman's voice singing old songs
with new words, with a quiet bass, a flute
plucked and fingered by women outside the law.

XIV

It was your vision of the pilot
confirmed my vision of you: you said, *He keeps
on steering headlong into the waves, on purpose*
while we crouched in the open hatchway
vomiting into plastic bags
for three hours between St. Pierre and Miquelon.
I never felt closer to you.
In the close cabin where the honeymoon couples
huddled in each other's laps and arms

I put my hand on your thigh
to comfort both of us, your hand came over mine,
we stayed that way, suffering together
in our bodies, as if all suffering
were physical, we touched so in the presence
of strangers who knew nothing and cared less
vomiting their private pain
as if all suffering were physical.

(THE FLOATING POEM, UNNUMBERED)

Whatever happens with us, your body
will haunt mine—tender, delicate
your lovemaking, like the half-curled frond
of the fiddlehead fern in forests
just washed by sun. Your traveled, generous thighs
between which my whole face has come and come—
the innocence and wisdom of the place my tongue has found there—
the live, insatiate dance of your nipples in my mouth—
your touch on me, firm, protective, searching
me out, your strong tongue and slender fingers
reaching where I had been waiting years for you
in my rose-wet cave—whatever happens, this is.

XV

If I lay on that beach with you
white, empty, pure green water warmed by the Gulf Stream
and lying on that beach we could not stay
because the wind drove fine sand against us
as if it were against us
if we tried to withstand it and we failed—
if we drove to another place
to sleep in each other's arms
and the beds were narrow like prisoners' cots
and we were tired and did not sleep together

and this was what we found, so this is what we did—
was the failure ours?
If I cling to circumstances I could feel
not responsible. Only she who says
she did not choose, is the loser in the end.

XVI

Across a city from you, I'm with you,
just as an August night
moony, inlet-warm, seabathed, I watched you sleep,
the scrubbed, sheenless wood of the dressing-table
cluttered with our brushes, books, vials in the moonlight—
or a salt-mist orchard, lying at your side
watching red sunset through the screendoor of the cabin,
G minor Mozart on the tape-recorder,
falling asleep to the music of the sea.
This island of Manhattan is wide enough
for both of us, and narrow:
I can hear your breath tonight, I know how your face
lies upturned, the halflight tracing
your generous, delicate mouth
where grief and laughter sleep together.

XVII

No one's fated or doomed to love anyone.
The accidents happen, we're not heroines,
they happen in our lives like car crashes,
books that change us, neighborhoods
we move into and come to love.
Tristan und Isolde is scarcely the story,
women at least should know the difference
between love and death. No poison cup,
no penance. Merely a notion that the tape-recorder
should have caught some ghost of us: that tape-recorder

not merely played but should have listened to us,
and could instruct those after us:
this we were, this is how we tried to love,
and these are the forces they had ranged against us,
and these are the forces we had ranged within us,
within us and against us, against us and within us.

XVIII

Rain on the West Side Highway,
red light at Riverside:
the more I live the more I think
two people together is a miracle.
You're telling the story of your life
for once, a tremor breaks the surface of your words.
The story of our lives becomes our lives.
Now you're in fugue across what some I'm sure
Victorian poet called the *salt estranging sea.*
Those are the words that come to mind.
I feel estrangement, yes. As I've felt dawn
pushing toward daybreak. Something: a cleft of light—?
Close between grief and anger, a space opens
where I am Adrienne alone. And growing colder.

XIX

Can it be growing colder when I begin
to touch myself again, adhesions pull away?
When slowly the naked face turns from staring backward
and looks into the present,
the eye of winter, city, anger, poverty, and death
and the lips part and say: *I mean to go on living?*
Am I speaking coldly when I tell you in a dream
or in this poem, *There are no miracles?*
(I told you from the first I wanted daily life,
this island of Manhattan was island enough for me.)

If I could let you know—
two women together is a work
nothing in civilization has made simple,
two people together is a work
heroic in its ordinariness,
the slow-picked, halting traverse of a pitch
where the fiercest attention becomes routine
—look at the faces of those who have chosen it.

XX

That conversation we were always on the edge
of having, runs on in my head,
at night the Hudson trembles in New Jersey light
polluted water yet reflecting even
sometimes the moon
and I discern a woman
I loved, drowning in secrets, fear wound round her throat
and choking her like hair. And this is she
with whom I tried to speak, whose hurt, expressive head
turning aside from pain, is dragged down deeper
where it cannot hear me,
and soon I shall know I was talking to my own soul.

XXI

The dark lintels, the blue and foreign stones
of the great round rippled by stone implements
the midsummer night light rising from beneath
the horizon—when I said "a cleft of light"
I meant this. And this is not Stonehenge
simply nor any place but the mind
casting back to where her solitude,
shared, could be chosen without loneliness,
not easily nor without pains to stake out

the circle, the heavy shadows, the great light.
I choose to be a figure in that light,
half-blotted by darkness, something moving
across that space, the color of stone
greeting the moon, yet more than stone:
a woman. I choose to walk here. And to draw this circle.

1974–1976

III

NOT
SOMEWHERE
ELSE,
BUT HERE

NOT SOMEWHERE ELSE, BUT HERE

Courage   Her face in the leaves   the polygons
of the paving   Her   out of touch
Courage to breathe   The death of October
Spilt wine   The unbuilt house   The unmade life
Graffiti   without memory   grown conventional
scrawling the least wall   *god loves you   voice of the ghetto*
Death of the city   Her face
sleeping   Her quick stride   Her
running   Search for a private space   The city
caving in from within   The lessons badly
learned   Or not at all   The unbuilt world
This one love flowing   Touching other
lives   Spilt love   The least wall caving

To have enough courage   The life that must be lived
in terrible October
Sudden immersion in yellows   streaked blood   The fast rain
Faces   Inscriptions   Trying to teach
unlearnable lessons   October   This one love
Repetitions   from other lives   The deaths
that must be lived   Denials   Blank walls
Our quick stride side by side   Her fugue

Bad air in the tunnels   *voice of the ghetto   god loves you*
My face   pale in the window   anger is pale
the blood shrinks to the heart
the head severed   it does not pay to feel

Her face   The fast rain tearing   Courage
to feel this   To tell of this   to be alive

Trying to learn   unteachable lessons

The fugue   Blood in my eyes   The careful sutures
ripped open   The hands that touch me   Shall it be said
I am not alone
Spilt love   seeking its level   flooding other
lives   that must be lived   not somewhere else
but here   seeing through blood   nothing is lost

1974

UPPER BROADWAY

The leafbud straggles forth
toward the frigid light of the airshaft   this is faith
this pale extension of a day
when looking up   you know   something is changing
winter has turned   though the wind is colder
Three streets away   a roof collapses   onto people
who thought they still had time   Time out of mind

I have written so many words
wanting to live inside you
to be of use to you

Now I must write for myself   for this blind
woman scratching the pavement   with her wand of thought
this slippered crone   inching on icy streets
reaching into wire trashbaskets   pulling out
what was thrown away   and infinitely precious

I look at my hands and see   they are still unfinished
I look at the vine and see the leafbud
inching towards life

I look at my face in the glass   and see
a halfborn woman

1975

PAULA BECKER TO CLARA WESTHOFF

Paula Becker 1876–1907
Clara Westhoff 1878–1954

became friends at Worpswede, an artists' colony near
Bremen, Germany, summer 1899. In January 1900, spent
a half-year together in Paris, where Paula painted and Clara
studied sculpture with Rodin. In August they returned to
Worpswede, and spent the next winter together in Berlin.
In 1901, Clara married the poet Rainer Maria Rilke; soon
after, Paula married the painter Otto Modersohn. She died
in a hemorrhage after childbirth, murmuring, *What a shame!*

The autumn feels slowed down,
summer still holds on here, even the light
seems to last longer than it should
or maybe I'm using it to the thin edge.
The moon rolls in the air. I didn't want this child.
You're the only one I've told.
I want a child maybe, someday, but not now.
Otto has a calm, complacent way
of following me with his eyes, as if to say
Soon you'll have your hands full!
And yes, I will; this child will be mine
not his, the failures, if I fail
will be all mine. We're not good, Clara,
at learning to prevent these things,
and once we have a child, it *is* ours.
But lately, I feel beyond Otto or anyone.
I know now the kind of work I have to do.
It takes such energy! I have the feeling I'm
moving somewhere, patiently, impatiently,
in my loneliness. I'm looking everywhere in nature
for new forms, old forms in new places,
the planes of an antique mouth, let's say, among the leaves.
I know and do not know
what I am searching for.
Remember those months in the studio together,

you up to your strong forearms in wet clay,
I trying to make something of the strange impressions
assailing me—the Japanese
flowers and birds on silk, the drunks
sheltering in the Louvre, that river-light,
those faces. . . . Did we know exactly
why we were there? Paris unnerved you,
you found it too much, yet you went on
with your work . . . and later we met there again,
both married then, and I thought you and Rilke
both seemed unnerved. I felt a kind of joylessness
between you. Of course he and I
have had our difficulties. Maybe I was jealous
of him, to begin with, taking you from me,
maybe I married Otto to fill up
my loneliness for you.
Rainer, of course, *knows* more than Otto knows,
he believes in women. But he feeds on us,
like all of them. His whole life, his art
is protected by women. Which of us could say that?
Which of us, Clara, hasn't had to take that leap
out beyond our being women
to save our work? or is it to save ourselves?
Marriage is lonelier than solitude.
Do you know: I was dreaming I had died
giving birth to the child.
I couldn't paint or speak or even move.
My child—I think—survived me. But what was funny
in the dream was, Rainer had written my requiem—
a long, beautiful poem, and calling me his friend.
I was *your* friend
but in the dream you didn't say a word.
In the dream his poem was like a letter
to someone who has no right
to be there but must be treated gently, like a guest

who comes on the wrong day. Clara, why don't I dream of you?
That photo of the two of us—I have it still,
you and I looking hard into each other
and my painting behind us. How we used to work
side by side! And how I've worked since then
trying to create according to our plan
that we'd bring, against all odds, our full power
to every subject. Hold back nothing
because we were women. Clara, our strength still lies
in the things we used to talk about:
how life and death take one another's hands,
the struggle for truth, our old pledge against guilt.
And now I feel dawn and the coming day.
I love waking in my studio, seeing my pictures
come alive in the light. Sometimes I feel
it is myself that kicks inside me,
myself I must give suck to, love . . .
I wish we could have done this for each other
all our lives, but we can't . . .
They say a pregnant woman
dreams of her own death. But life and death
take one another's hands. Clara, I feel so full
of work, the life I see ahead, and love
for you, who of all people
however badly I say this
will hear all I say and cannot say.

1975–1976

NIGHTS AND DAYS

The stars will come out over and over
the hyacinths rise like flames
from the windswept turf down the middle of upper Broadway
where the desolate take the sun
the days will run together and stream into years
as the rivers freeze and burn
and I ask myself and you, which of our visions will claim us
which will we claim
how will we go on living
how will we touch, what will we know
what will we say to each other.

Pictures form and dissolve in my head:
we are walking in a city
you fled, came back to and come back to still
which I saw once through winter frost
years back, before I knew you,
before I knew myself.
We are walking streets you have by heart from childhood
streets you have graven and erased in dreams:
scrolled portals, trees, nineteenth-century statues.
We are holding hands so I can see
everything as you see it
I follow you into your dreams
your past, the places
none of us can explain to anyone.

We are standing in the wind
on an empty beach, the onslaught of the surf
tells me Point Reyes, or maybe some northern
Pacific shoreline neither of us has seen.
In its fine spectral mist our hair

is grey as the sea
someone who saw us far-off would say we were two old women
Norns, perhaps, or sisters of the spray
but our breasts are beginning to sing together
your eyes are on my mouth

I wake early in the morning
in a bed we have shared for years
lie watching your innocent, sacred sleep
as if for the first time.
We have been together so many nights and days
this day is not unusual.
I walk to an eastern window, pull up the blinds:
the city around us is still
on a clear October morning
wrapped in her indestructible light.

The stars will come out over and over
the hyacinths rise like flames
from the windswept turf down the middle of upper Broadway
where the desolate take the sun
the days will run together and stream into years
as the rivers freeze and burn
and I ask myself and you, which of our visions will claim us
which will we claim
how will we go on living
how will we touch, what will we know
what will we say to each other.

1976

SIBLING MYSTERIES

(FOR C. R.)

1.

Remind me how we walked
trying the planetary rock
for foothold

testing the rims of canyons
fields of sheer
ice in the midnight sun

smelling the rains before they came
feeling the fullness of the moon
before moonrise

unbalanced by the life
moving in us, then lightened
yet weighted still

by children on our backs
at our hips, as we made fire
scooped clay   lifted water

Remind me how the stream
wetted the clay between our palms
and how the flame

licked it to mineral colors
how we traced our signs by torchlight
in the deep chambers of the caves

and how we drew the quills

of porcupines between our teeth
to a keen thinness

and brushed the twisted raffia into velvet
and bled our lunar knowledge thirteen times
upon the furrows

I know by heart, and still
I need to have you tell me,
hold me, remind me

2.
Remind me how we loved our mother's body
our mouths drawing the first
thin sweetness from her nipples

our faces dreaming hour on hour
in the salt smell of her lap   Remind me
how her touch melted childgrief

how she floated great and tender in our dark
or stood guard over us
against our willing

and how we thought she loved
the strange male body first
that took, that took, whose taking seemed a law

and how she sent us weeping
into that law
how we remet her in our childbirth visions

erect, enthroned, above
a spiral stair
and crawled and panted toward her

I know, I remember, but
hold me, remind me
of how her woman's flesh was made taboo to us

3.
And how beneath the veil
black gauze or white, the dragging
bangles, the amulets, we dreamed   And how beneath

the strange male bodies
we sank in terror or in resignation
and how we taught them tenderness—

the holding-back, the play,
the floating of a finger
the secrets of the nipple

And how we ate and drank
their leavings, how we served them
in silence, how we told

among ourselves our secrets, wept and laughed
passed bark and root and berry
from hand to hand, whispering each one's power

washing the bodies of the dead
making celebrations of doing laundry
piecing our lore in quilted galaxies

how we dwelt in two worlds
the daughters and the mothers
in the kingdom of the sons

4.
Tell me again because I need to hear

how we bore our mother-secrets
straight to the end

tied in unlawful rags
between our breasts
muttered in blood

in looks exchanged at the feast
where the fathers sucked the bones
and struck their bargains

in the open square when noon
battered our shaven heads
and the flames curled transparent in the sun

in boats of skin on the ice-floe
—the pregnant set to drift,
too many mouths for feeding—

how sister gazed at sister
reaching through mirrored pupils
back to the mother

5.
C. had a son on June 18th . . . I feel acutely that we are strangers, my sis-
ter and I; we don't get through to each other, or say what we really feel.
This depressed me violently on that occasion, when I wanted to have only
generous and simple feelings towards her, of pleasure in her joy, affection
for all that was hers. But we are not really friends, and act the part of sis-
ters. I don't know what really gives her pain or joy, nor does she know how
I am happy or how I suffer.

(1963)

There were years you and I
hardly spoke to each other

then one whole night
our father dying upstairs

we burned our childhood, reams of paper,
talking till the birds sang

Your face across a table now: dark
with illumination

This face I have watched changing
for forty years

has watched me changing
this mind has wrenched my thought

I feel the separateness
of cells in us, split-second choice

of one ovum for one sperm?
We have seized different weapons

our hair has fallen long
or short at different times

words flash from you I never thought of
we are translations into different dialects

of a text still being written
in the original

yet our eyes drink from each other
our lives were driven down the same dark canal

6.
We have returned so far
that house of childhood seems absurd

its secrets a fallen hair, a grain of dust
on the photographic plate

we are eternally exposing to the universe
I call you from another planet

to tell a dream
Light-years away, you weep with me

The daughters never were
true brides of the father

the daughters were to begin with
brides of the mother

then brides of each other
under a different law

Let me hold and tell you

1976

A WOMAN DEAD IN HER FORTIES

1.

Your breasts/   sliced-off   The scars
dimmed   as they would have to be
years later

All the women I grew up with are sitting
half-naked on rocks   in sun
we look at each other and
are not ashamed

and you too have taken off your blouse
but this was not what you wanted:

to show your scarred, deleted torso

I barely glance at you
as if my look could scald you
though I'm the one who loved you

I want to touch my fingers
to where your breasts had been
but we never did such things

You hadn't thought everyone
would look so perfect
unmutilated

you pull on
your blouse again: stern statement:

There are things I will not share
with everyone

2.
You send me back to share
my own scars   first of all
with myself

What did I hide from her
what have I denied her
what losses suffered

how in this ignorant body
did she hide

waiting for her release
till uncontrollable light began to pour

from every wound and suture
and all the sacred openings

3.
Wartime.   We sit on warm
weathered, softening grey boards

the ladder glimmers where you told me
the leeches swim

I smell the flame
of kerosene   the pine

boards where we sleep side by side
in narrow cots

the night-meadow exhaling
its darkness   calling

child into woman
child into woman
woman

4.
Most of our love from the age of nine
took the form of jokes and mute

loyalty: you fought a girl
who said she'd knock me down

we did each other's homework
wrote letters   kept in touch, untouching

lied about our lives: I wearing
the face of the proper marriage

you the face of the independent woman
We cleaved to each other across that space

fingering webs
of love and estrangement   till the day

the gynecologist touched your breast
and found a palpable hardness

5.
You played heroic, necessary
games with death

since in your neo-protestant tribe the void
was supposed not to exist

except as a fashionable concept

you had no traffic with

I wish you were here tonight   I want
to yell at you

Don't accept
Don't give in

But would I be meaning your brave
irreproachable life, you dean of women, or

your unfair, unfashionable, unforgivable
woman's death?

6.
You are every woman I ever loved
and disavowed

a bloody incandescent chord strung out
across years, tracts of space

How can I reconcile this passion
with our modesty

your calvinist heritage
my girlhood frozen into forms

how can I go on this mission
without you

you, who might have told me
everything you feel is true?

7.
Time after time in dreams you rise
reproachful

once from a wheelchair pushed by your father
across a lethal expressway

Of all my dead it's you
who come to me unfinished

You left me amber beads
strung with turquoise from an Egyptian grave

I wear them wondering
How am I true to you?

I'm half-afraid to write poetry
for you   who never read it much

and I'm left laboring
with the secrets and the silence

In plain language: I never told you how I loved you
we never talked at your deathbed of your death

8.
One autumn evening in a train
catching the diamond-flash of sunset

in puddles along the Hudson
I thought: *I understand*

life and death now, the choices

I didn't know your choice

or how by then you had no choice
how the body tells the truth in its rush of cells

Most of our love took the form
of mute loyalty

we never spoke at your deathbed of your death

but from here on
I want more crazy mourning, more howl, more keening

We stayed mute and disloyal
because we were afraid

I would have touched my fingers
to where your breasts had been
but we never did such things

1974–1977

MOTHER-RIGHT

(FOR M. H.)

Woman and child   running
in a field   A man planted
on the horizon

Two hands   one long, slim   one
small, starlike   clasped
in the razor wind

Her hair cut short for faster travel
the child's curls grazing his shoulders
the hawk-winged cloud   over their heads

The man is walking boundaries
measuring   He believes in what is his
the grass   the waters underneath   the air

the air   through which child and mother
are running   the boy singing
the woman   eyes sharpened in the light
heart stumbling   making for the open

1977

NATURAL RESOURCES

1.
The core of the strong hill: not understood:
the mulch-heat of the underwood

where unforeseen the forest fire unfurls;
the heat, the privacy of the mines;

the rainbow laboring to extend herself
where neither men nor cattle understand,

arching her lusters over rut and stubble
purely to reach where she must go;

the emerald lying against the silver vein
waiting for light to reach it, breathing in pain;

the miner laboring beneath
the ray of the headlamp: a weight like death.

2.
The miner is no metaphor. She goes
into the cage like the rest, is flung

downward by gravity like them, must change
her body like the rest to fit a crevice

to work a lode
on her the pick hangs heavy, the bad air

lies thick, the mountain presses in on her
with boulder, timber, fog

slowly the mountain's dust descends
into the fibers of her lungs.

3.
The cage drops into the dark,
the routine of life goes on:

a woman turns a doorknob, but so slowly
so quietly, that no one wakes

and it is she alone who gazes
into the dark of bedrooms, ascertains

how they sleep, who needs her touch
what window blows the ice of February

into the room and who must be protected:
It is only she who sees; who was trained to see.

4.
Could you imagine a world of women only,
the interviewer asked. *Can you imagine*

a world where women are absent. (He believed
he was joking.) *Yet I have to imagine*

at once and the same moment, both. Because
I live in both. *Can you imagine,*

the interviewer asked, *a world of men?*
(He thought he was joking.) *If so, then,*

a world where men are absent?
Absently, wearily, I answered: Yes.

5.
The phantom of the man-who-would-understand,
the lost brother, the twin—

for him did we leave our mothers,
deny our sisters, over and over?

did we invent him, conjure him
over the charring log,

nights, late, in the snowbound cabin
did we dream or scry his face

in the liquid embers,
the man-who-would-dare-to-know-us?

6.
It was never the rapist:
it was the brother, lost,

the comrade/twin whose palm
would bear a lifeline like our own:

decisive, arrowy,
forked-lightning of insatiate desire

It was never the crude pestle, the blind
ramrod we were after:

merely a fellow-creature
with natural resources equal to our own

7.
Meanwhile, another kind of being
was constructing itself, blindly

—a mutant, some have said:
the blood-compelled exemplar

of a "botched civilization"
as one of them called it

children picking up guns
for that is what it means to be a man

We have lived with violence for seven years
It was not worth one single life—

but the patriot's fist is at her throat,
her voice is in mortal danger

and that kind of being has lain in our beds
declaring itself our desire

requiring women's blood for life
a woman's breast to lay its nightmare on

8.
And that kind of being has other forms:
a passivity we mistake

—in the desperation of our search—
for gentleness

But gentleness is active
gentleness swabs the crusted stump

invents more merciful instruments
to touch the wound beyond the wound

does not faint with disgust

will not be driven off

keeps bearing witness calmly
against the predator, the parasite

9.
I am tired of faintheartedness,
their having to be *exceptional*

to do what an ordinary woman
does in the course of things

I am tired of women stooping to half our height
to bring the essential vein to light

tired of the waste of what we bear
with such cost, such elation, into sight

(—for what becomes of what the miner probes
and carves from the mountain's body in her pain?)

10.
This is what I am: watching the spider
rebuild—"patiently", they say,

but I recognize in her
impatience—my own—

the passion to make and make again
where such unmaking reigns

the refusal to be a victim
we have lived with violence so long

Am I to go on saying
for myself, for her

This is my body,
take and destroy it?

11.
The enormity of the simplest things:
in this cold barn tables are spread

with china saucers, shoehorns
of german silver, a gilt-edged book

that opens into a picture-frame
a biscuit-tin of the thirties.

Outside, the north lies vast
with unshed snow, everything is

at once remote and familiar
each house contains what it must

women simmer carcasses
of clean-picked turkeys, store away

the cleaned cutglass and soak the linen cloths
Dark rushes early at the panes

12.
These things by women saved
are all we have of them

or of those dear to them
these ribboned letters, snapshots

faithfully glued for years
onto the scrapbook page

these scraps, turned into patchwork,
doll-gowns, clean white rags

for stanching blood
the bride's tea-yellow handkerchief

the child's height penciled on the cellar door
In this cold barn we dream

a universe of humble things—
and without these, no memory

no faithfulness, no purpose for the future
no honor to the past

13.
There are words I cannot choose again:
humanism   androgyny

Such words have no shame in them, no diffidence
before the raging stoic grandmothers:

their glint is too shallow, like a dye
that does not permeate

the fibers of actual life
as we live it, now:

this fraying blanket with its ancient stains
we pull across the sick child's shoulder

or wrap around the senseless legs
of the hero trained to kill

this weaving, ragged because incomplete
we turn our hands to, interrupted

over and over, handed down
unfinished, found in the drawer

of an old dresser in the barn,
her vanished pride and care

still urging us, urging on
our work, to close the gap

in the Great Nebula,
to help the earth deliver.

14.
The women who first knew themselves
miners, are dead. The rainbow flies

like a flying buttress from the walls
of cloud, the silver-and-green vein

awaits the battering of the pick
the dark lode weeps for light

My heart is moved by all I cannot save:
so much has been destroyed

I have to cast my lot with those
who age after age, perversely,

with no extraordinary power,
reconstitute the world.

1977

TOWARD THE SOLSTICE

The thirtieth of November.
Snow is starting to fall.
A peculiar silence is spreading
over the fields, the maple grove.
It is the thirtieth of May,
rain pours on ancient bushes, runs
down the youngest blade of grass.
I am trying to hold in one steady glance
all the parts of my life.
A spring torrent races
on this old slanting roof,
the slanted field below
thickens with winter's first whiteness.
Thistles dried to sticks in last year's wind
stand nakedly in the green,
stand sullenly in the slowly whitening,
field.

       My brain glows
more violently, more avidly
the quieter, the thicker
the quilt of crystals settles,
the louder, more relentlessly
the torrent beats itself out
on the old boards and shingles.
It is the thirtieth of May,
the thirtieth of November,
a beginning or an end,
we are moving into the solstice
and there is so much here
I still do not understand.

If I could make sense of how
my life is still tangled
with dead weeds, thistles,
enormous burdocks, burdens
slowly shifting under
this first fall of snow,
beaten by this early, racking rain
calling all new life to declare itself strong
or die,
            if I could know
in what language to address
the spirits that claim a place
beneath these low and simple ceilings,
tenants that neither speak nor stir
yet dwell in mute insistence
till I can feel utterly ghosted in this house.

If history is a spider-thread
spun over and over though brushed away
it seems I might some twilight
or dawn in the hushed country light
discern its greyness stretching
from molding or doorframe, out
into the empty dooryard
and following it climb
the path into the pinewoods,
tracing from tree to tree
in the failing light, in the slowly
lucidifying day
its constant, purposive trail,
till I reach whatever cellar hole
filling with snowflakes or lichen,
whatever fallen shack
or unremembered clearing
I am meant to have found

and there, under the first or last
star, trusting to instinct
the words would come to mind
I have failed or forgotten to say
year after year, winter
after summer, the right rune
to ease the hold of the past
upon the rest of my life
and ease my hold on the past.

If some rite of separation
is still unaccomplished
between myself and the long-gone
tenants of this house,
between myself and my childhood,
and the childhood of my children,
it is I who have neglected
to perform the needed acts,
set water in corners, light and eucalyptus
in front of mirrors,
or merely pause and listen
to my own pulse vibrating
lightly as falling snow,
relentlessly as the rainstorm,
and hear what it has been saying.
It seems I am still waiting
for them to make some clear demand
some articulate sound or gesture,
for release to come from anywhere
but from inside myself.

A decade of cutting away
dead flesh, cauterizing
old scars ripped open over and over
and still it is not enough.

A decade of performing
the loving humdrum acts
of attention to this house
transplanting lilac suckers,
washing panes, scrubbing
wood-smoke from splitting paint,
sweeping stairs, brushing the thread
of the spider aside,
and so much yet undone,
a woman's work, the solstice nearing,
and my hand still suspended
as if above a letter
I long and dread to close.

1977

TRANSCENDENTAL ETUDE

(FOR MICHELLE CLIFF)

This August evening I've been driving
over backroads fringed with queen anne's lace
my car startling young deer in meadows—one
gave a hoarse intake of her breath and all
four fawns sprang after her
into the dark maples.
Three months from today they'll be fair game
for the hit-and-run hunters, glorying
in a weekend's destructive power,
triggers fingered by drunken gunmen, sometimes
so inept as to leave the shattered animal
stunned in her blood. But this evening deep in summer
the deer are still alive and free,
nibbling apples from early-laden boughs
so weighted, so englobed
with already yellowing fruit
they seem eternal, Hesperidean
in the clear-tuned, cricket-throbbing air.

Later I stood in the dooryard,
my nerves singing the immense
fragility of all this sweetness,
this green world already sentimentalized, photographed,
advertised to death. Yet, it persists
stubbornly beyond the fake Vermont
of antique barnboards glazed into discothèques,
artificial snow, the sick Vermont of children
conceived in apathy, grown to winters
of rotgut violence,
poverty gnashing its teeth like a blind cat at their lives.
Still, it persists. Turning off onto a dirt road

from the raw cuts bulldozed through a quiet village
for the tourist run to Canada,
I've sat on a stone fence above a great, soft, sloping field
of musing heifers, a farmstead
slanting its planes calmly in the calm light,
a dead elm raising bleached arms
above a green so dense with life,
minute, momentary life—slugs, moles, pheasants, gnats,
spiders, moths, hummingbirds, groundhogs, butterflies—
a lifetime is too narrow
to understand it all, beginning with the huge
rockshelves that underlie all that life.

No one ever told us we had to study our lives,
make of our lives a study, as if learning natural history
or music, that we should begin
with the simple exercises first
and slowly go on trying
the hard ones, practicing till strength
and accuracy became one with the daring
to leap into transcendence, take the chance
of breaking down in the wild arpeggio
or faulting the full sentence of the fugue.
—And in fact we can't live like that: we take on
everything at once before we've even begun
to read or mark time, we're forced to begin
in the midst of the hardest movement,
the one already sounding as we are born.
At most we're allowed a few months
of simply listening to the simple line
of a woman's voice singing a child
against her heart. Everything else is too soon,
too sudden, the wrenching-apart, that woman's heartbeat
heard ever after from a distance,

the loss of that ground-note echoing
whenever we are happy, or in despair.

Everything else seems beyond us,
we aren't ready for it, nothing that was said
is true for us, caught naked in the argument,
the counterpoint, trying to sightread
what our fingers can't keep up with, learn by heart
what we can't even read. And yet
it *is* this we were born to. We aren't virtuosi
or child prodigies, there are no prodigies
in this realm, only a half-blind, stubborn
cleaving to the timbre, the tones of what we are
—even when all the texts describe it differently.

And we're not performers, like Liszt, competing
against the world for speed and brilliance
(the 79-year-old pianist said, when I asked her
What makes a virtuoso?—Competitiveness.)
The longer I live the more I mistrust
theatricality, the false glamour cast
by performance, the more I know its poverty beside
the truths we are salvaging from
the splitting-open of our lives.
The woman who sits watching, listening,
eyes moving in the darkness
is rehearsing in her body, hearing-out in her blood
a score touched off in her perhaps
by some words, a few chords, from the stage:
a tale only she can tell.

But there come times—perhaps this is one of them—
when we have to take ourselves more seriously or die;
when we have to pull back from the incantations,
rhythms we've moved to thoughtlessly,

and disenthrall ourselves, bestow
ourselves to silence, or a severer listening, cleansed
of oratory, formulas, choruses, laments, static
crowding the wires. We cut the wires,
find ourselves in free-fall, as if
our true home were the undimensional
solitudes, the rift
in the Great Nebula.
No one who survives to speak
new language, has avoided this:
the cutting-away of an old force that held her
rooted to an old ground
the pitch of utter loneliness
where she herself and all creation
seem equally dispersed, weightless, her being a cry
to which no echo comes or can ever come.

But in fact we were always like this,
rootless, dismembered: knowing it makes the difference.
Birth stripped our birthright from us,
tore us from a woman, from women, from ourselves
so early on
and the whole chorus throbbing at our ears
like midges, told us nothing, nothing
of origins, nothing we needed
to know, nothing that could re member us.

Only: that it is unnatural,
the homesickness for a woman, for ourselves,
for that acute joy at the shadow her head and arms
cast on a wall, her heavy or slender
thighs on which we lay, flesh against flesh,
eyes steady on the face of love; smell of her milk, her sweat,
terror of her disappearance, all fused in this hunger
for the element they have called most dangerous, to be

lifted breathtaken on her breast, to rock within her
—even if beaten back, stranded again, to apprehend
in a sudden brine-clear thought
trembling like the tiny, orbed, endangered
egg-sac of a new world:
This is what she was to me, and this
is how I can love myself—
as only a woman can love me.

Homesick for myself, for her—as, after the heatwave
breaks, the clear tones of the world
manifest: cloud, bough, wall, insect, the very soul of light:
homesick as the fluted vault of desire
articulates itself: *I am the lover and the loved,*
home and wanderer, she who splits
firewood and she who knocks, a stranger
in the storm, two women, eye to eye
measuring each other's spirit, each other's
limitless desire,
                    a whole new poetry beginning here.

Vision begins to happen in such a life
as if a woman quietly walked away
from the argument and jargon in a room
and sitting down in the kitchen, began turning in her lap
bits of yarn, calico and velvet scraps,
laying them out absently on the scrubbed boards
in the lamplight, with small rainbow-colored shells
sent in cotton-wool from somewhere far away,
and skeins of milkweed from the nearest meadow—
original domestic silk, the finest findings—
and the darkblue petal of the petunia,
and the dry darkbrown lace of seaweed;
not forgotten either, the shed silver
whisker of the cat,

the spiral of paper-wasp-nest curling
beside the finch's yellow feather.
Such a composition has nothing to do with eternity,
the striving for greatness, brilliance—
only with the musing of a mind
one with her body, experienced fingers quietly pushing
dark against bright, silk against roughness,
pulling the tenets of a life together
with no mere will to mastery,
only care for the many-lived, unending
forms in which she finds herself,
becoming now the sherd of broken glass
slicing light in a corner, dangerous
to flesh, now the plentiful, soft leaf
that wrapped round the throbbing finger, soothes the wound;
and now the stone foundation, rockshelf further
forming underneath everything that grows.

1977